On
Confidence

On
Confidence

The School of Life

Published in 2017 by The School of Life
First published in the USA in 2018
930 High Road, London, N12 9RT
Copyright © The School of Life 2017
Designed and typeset by Marcia Mihotich
Printed in Latvia by Livonia Print

A proportion of this book has appeared online at
www.theschooloflife.com/articles

Every effort has been made to contact the copyright holders of
the material reproduced in this book. If any have been
inadvertently overlooked, the publisher will be pleased to make
restitution at the earliest opportunity.

The School of Life publishes a range of books on essential topics
in psychological and emotional life, including relationships,
parenting, friendship, careers and fulfilment. The aim is always
to help us to understand ourselves better – and thereby to grow
calmer, less confused and more purposeful. Discover our full
range of titles, including books for children, here:
www.theschooloflife.com/books

The School of Life also offers a comprehensive therapy service,
which complements, and draws upon, our published works:
www.theschooloflife.com/therapy

www.theschooloflife.com

ISBN 978-0-9955736-7-3

20 19 18 17 16 15 14 13 12

MIX
Paper | Supporting
responsible forestry
FSC® C002795

Contents

I

Introduction

It can be humbling to realise just how many great achievements have not been the result of superior talent or technical know-how, merely that strange buoyancy of the soul we call confidence.

We spend vast amounts of time acquiring confidence in narrow technical fields: quadratic equations or bioengineering; economics or pole vaulting. But we overlook the primordial need to acquire a more free-ranging variety of confidence – one that can serve us across a range of tasks: speaking to strangers at parties, asking someone to marry us, suggesting a fellow passenger turn down their music, changing the world.

We so often lack confidence because we implicitly regard its possession as a matter of slightly freakish and irreplicable good luck. Some people simply are very confident, for reasons that neuroscientists may one day uncover. But, we tell ourselves, there isn't much we can do about our particular situation. We are stuck with the confidence levels we were born with.

In fact, the opposite is true. Confidence is a skill, not a gift from the gods. And it is a skill founded on a set of ideas about the world and our natural place within it.

Confidence is a skill, not a gift from the gods.

These ideas can be systematically studied and gradually learnt, so that the roots of excessive hesitancy and compliance can be overcome. We can school ourselves in the art of confidence.

II
Idiocy and Confidence

In well-meaning attempts to boost our confidence ahead of challenging moments, people often try to draw our attention to our strengths: our intelligence, our competence, our experience. However, this can have awkward consequences. There is a type of underconfidence that arises specifically when we grow too attached to our own dignity and become anxious around any situation that might seem to threaten it. We hold back from challenges in which there is any risk of ending up looking ridiculous – which comprises, of course, almost all the most interesting situations.

In a foreign city, we grow reluctant to ask anyone to guide us to the nice bars, because they might think us an ignorant, pitiable lost tourist. We might long to kiss someone, but never let on, in case they dismiss us as a predatory loser. At work, we don't apply for a promotion, in case the senior management deems us delusionally arrogant. In a concerted bid never to look foolish, we don't venture very far from our cocoon. Consequently – from time to time, at least – we miss out on the best opportunities of our lives.

At the heart of our underconfidence is a skewed picture of how dignified a normal person can be. We imagine that it might be possible, after a certain age, to place ourselves beyond mockery. We trust that it is an option to lead a good life without regularly making a complete idiot of ourselves.

One of the most charming books written in early modern Europe was *In Praise of Folly* (1509), by the Dutch scholar and philosopher Erasmus. In its pages, Erasmus advances a hugely liberating argument. In a warm tone, he reminds us that everyone, however important and learned they might seem, is a fool. No one is spared, not even the author. However well-schooled he himself was, Erasmus remained – he insists – as much of a nitwit as anyone else: his judgement is faulty; his passions get the better of him; he is prey to superstition and irrational fear; he is shy whenever he has to meet new people; he drops things at elegant dinners. This is deeply cheering, for it means that our own repeated idiocies do not have to exclude us from the best company. Looking like a prick, making blunders, and doing bizarre things in the night does not render us unfit for society; it makes us a little more like the greatest scholar of the northern European Renaissance.

There is a similarly uplifting message to be drawn from the work of Pieter Bruegel. His painting *Dutch Proverbs*

Pieter Bruegel the Elder, *Nederlandse Spreekwoorden (Dutch Proverbs)*, 1559.

presents a comically disenchanted view of human nature. Everyone, he suggests, is pretty much deranged: here's a man throwing his money into the river; there's a soldier squatting on the fire and burning his trousers; someone is intently bashing his head against a brick wall, someone else is biting a pillar. Importantly, the painting is not an attack on just a few unusually awful people: it is a picture of parts of all of us.

Bruegel and Erasmus's work proposes that the way to greater confidence is not to reassure ourselves of our own dignity; it's to come to peace with our inevitable ridiculousness. We are idiots now, we have been idiots in the past, and we will be idiots again in the future – and that's OK. There aren't any other available options for human beings.

We grow timid when we allow ourselves to be overexposed to the respectable sides of others. Such are the pains people take to appear normal, we collectively create a phantasm that suggests that normality might be possible, and this is problematic for everyone.

Once we learn to see ourselves as already, and by nature, foolish, it won't matter so much if we do one more thing that might look stupid. The person we try to kiss could indeed think us ridiculous. The individual from whom we asked directions in a foreign city might regard us with contempt. But if these people did so, it wouldn't be news to us. They would only be confirming what we had already gracefully accepted long ago: that we, like them – and every other person on the earth – are a nitwit. The risk of trying and failing would have its sting substantially removed. The fear of humiliation would no longer stalk us in the shadows of our minds. We would grow free to try things by accepting that failure was the norm. And every so often, amid the many rebuffs we would have factored in from the outset, it would work: we'd get a kiss, we'd make a friend, we'd get a raise.

The road to greater confidence begins with a ritual of telling oneself solemnly every morning, before heading out for the day, that one is a muttonhead, a cretin, a dumbbell and an imbecile. A few more acts of folly should, thereafter, not matter very much.

III
Impostor
Syndrome

Faced with challenges, we often leave the possibility of success to others, because we don't seem to ourselves to be the sort of people who win. When we approach the idea of acquiring responsibility or prestige, we quickly become convinced that we are 'impostors', like an actor in the role of a pilot, wearing the uniform and making sunny cabin announcements while incapable of even starting the engines.

The root cause of impostor syndrome is a hugely unhelpful picture of what people at the top of society are really like. We feel like impostors not because we are uniquely flawed, but because we can't imagine how deeply flawed the elite must also be beneath a more or less polished surface.

The impostor syndrome has its roots far back in childhood – specifically in the powerful sense children have that their parents are very different from them. To a four-year-old, it is incomprehensible that their mother was once their age and unable to drive a car, tell the plumber what to do, decide other people's bedtimes and go on trips with colleagues. The gulf in status appears absolute and unbridgeable. The child's passionate loves – bouncing on the sofa, Pingu, Toblerone – have nothing to do with those of adults, who like to sit at a table talking for hours and drinking beer that tastes like rusty metal. We start out in life with a very strong impression that competent and admirable people are not like us at all.

This childhood experience dovetails with a basic feature of the human condition. We know ourselves from the inside, but others only from the outside. We are aware of all our anxieties and doubts from within, yet all we know of others is what they happen to do and tell us – a far narrower and more edited source of information.

We are often left to conclude that we must be at the more freakish and revolting end of human nature. Really, however, we're just failing to imagine that others are every bit as fragile as we are. Without knowing what it is that troubles or wracks outwardly impressive people, we can be sure that it will be something. We might not know exactly what they regret, but there will be agonising feelings of some kind. We won't be able to say exactly what kind of sexual kink obsesses them, but there will be one. And we can know this because vulnerabilities and compulsions cannot be curses that have descended upon us uniquely; they are universal features of the human mental equipment.

The solution to the impostor syndrome lies in making a crucial leap of faith: that others' minds work in much the same way as ours do. Other people must be as anxious, uncertain and wayward as we are.

Traditionally, being a member of the aristocracy provided a fast track to confidence-giving knowledge about the true characters of the elite. In 18th-century England, an admiral of the Fleet would have looked deeply impressive to outsiders (more or less everyone), with his splendid uniform (cockaded hat, loads of gold) and thousands of subordinates to do his bidding. But to a young earl or marquis, who had moved in the same social circles all his life, the admiral would appear in a very different light. He would have seen him losing money at cards in the club the night before; he would know that his pet name in the nursery had been 'Sticky' because of his inept way of eating jam tarts; his aunt would still tell the story of the ridiculous way the admiral had tried to proposition her sister in the Yew Walk; he would know the admiral was in debt to his grandfather, who regarded him as pretty dim. Through acquaintance, the aristocrat would have reached a wise awareness that being an admiral was not an unattainable position reserved for gods; it was the sort of thing Sticky could do.

The solution to the impostor syndrome lies in making a crucial leap of faith.

The other traditional release from underconfidence of this type came from the opposite end of the social spectrum: being a servant. 'No man is a hero to his valet,' remarked the 16th-century French essayist Montaigne – a lack of respect that may at points prove deeply encouraging, given how much our awe can sap our will to rival or match our heroes. Great public figures aren't ever so impressive to those who look after them, who see them drunk in the early hours, examine the stains on their underpants, hear their secret misgivings about matters on which they publicly hold firm views and witness them weeping with shame over the strategic blunders they officially deny.

The valet and the aristocrat reasonably and automatically grasp the limitations of the authority of the elite. Fortunately, we don't have to be either one to liberate ourselves from inhibiting degrees of respect for the powerful; imagination will serve just as well. One of the tasks that works of art should ideally accomplish is to take us more reliably into the minds of people we are intimidated by and show us the more average, muddled and fretful experiences unfolding inside.

At another point in his *Essays* of 1580, Montaigne playfully informed his readers in plain French that: 'Kings and philosophers shit and so do ladies'. Montaigne's thesis is that, for all the evidence that exists about this shitting, we might not guess that grand people ever had to squat on a toilet. We never see distinguished types doing this – while we, of course, are immensely well informed of our own digestive activities. Therefore, we build up a sense that because we have crude and sometimes rather desperate bodies, we can't be philosophers, kings or ladies; and that if we set ourselves up in these roles, we'd just be impostors.

With Montaigne's guidance, we are invited to take on a saner sense of what powerful people are actually like. But the real target isn't just an underconfidence about bodily functions; it is psychological timidity. Montaigne might have said that kings, philosophers and ladies are wracked by self-doubt and feelings of inadequacy, sometimes bump into doors and have weird lustful thoughts about members of their own families. Furthermore, instead of considering only the big figures of 16th-century France, we could update the example and refer to CEOs, corporate lawyers, news presenters and successful startup entrepreneurs. They too can't cope, feel they might buckle under pressure and look back on certain decisions with shame and regret. No less than shitting, such feelings belong to us all. Our inner frailties don't cut us off from doing what they do. If we were in their roles, we'd not be impostors, we would simply be normal.

Making a leap of faith around what other people are like helps to humanise the world. Whenever we encounter a stranger, we are not really encountering such a person; we are encountering someone who is in basic ways very much like us, despite surface evidence to the contrary. Therefore, nothing fundamental stands between us and the possibility of responsibility, success and fulfilment.

IV
Trust in the
System

When we take our ideas out into the world, there is no more common response than to hear a 'no' in return.

We develop a proposal at work that seems pretty good to us. We do some research, put together strategic options and hand it to a senior colleague who agrees to give it some thought. Then, after six weeks, a message comes back: the firm is grateful for the suggestion, but won't be taking the plan further. There is no very precise explanation, just a general view: the timing is wrong; it doesn't fit with general policy; it's not the kind of thing that's right for the team. We may be disappointed, but we take the comments on the chin. Our suggestion couldn't really have been a good one. Perhaps we should be more careful in the future.

Or maybe we've hit upon an idea for a new kind of product. It looks to us as if there might be a significant gap in the market. We call in a business advisor and talk it through. But they tell us, with a striking degree of sarcasm, that it's not going to work. They wear very elegant spectacles and once worked with BMW and Google. Later, we delete the whole presentation from our laptop.

Or, perhaps for years, we've been happily using our old

phone. It's not terribly sophisticated but it does just the things we want. Unfortunately, we leave it on a train. At the shop, they're not at all helpful. They tell us our model is absurdly outdated, equipped with a stone-age processor and a 960 x 540-pixel resolution display that doesn't respond well to any of the new swipe commands. There's nothing to be done. We accept the suggestion of a phone we don't like so much. Then, a few weeks later, at a conference, we see someone happily using exactly the phone we wanted.

In big and small instances, we cave in to the judgements of The System, beside whose might and invincibility our own hopes seem feeble and disposable. The root of our underconfidence is a touching, but ultimately hugely dangerous, degree of trust – a legacy of times in our lives when those in charge had our best interests in mind and took the time to assess every one of our needs. When a parent told us we couldn't use the computer in our bedroom or that it wasn't advisable for us to go on the school trip to Spain, we could trust that they weren't being merely mean or unimaginative; they were the bearers of bad news out of mature benevolence.

From such experiences, we may develop a more generalised

belief in the open-heartedness of those who frustrate us. The senior manager, business advisor or sales assistant are, we feel, in their own ways as careful about their judgements as our own families. But this, of course, can't be true.

At the end of the Classical period, on the cusp of the 4th and 5th centuries of the modern era, as the Roman Empire in the West was collapsing, the Christian philosopher St. Augustine tried to describe the essential, unavoidable flaws of all human systems. He drew a fundamental contrast between two realms. One he called the City of God, an imagined ideal in which institutions could be exactly the way we'd like them to be: wise, altruistic and benign. On the other hand, there was what he called the City of Man, a realm that described institutions as they actually were: occasionally well-meaning, but frequently lazy, casual, corrupt or indifferent.

The dark brilliancy of Augustine's diagnosis was his conviction that it would by nature be impossible for human institutions ever to meet our hopes. They could never be the wise and kindly organisations that they presented themselves as being. Such aspirations belonged to what

Maturity means going from the myth of a person to a full recognition of their humanity.

he thought of as the afterlife – or, as we might now more reasonably put it, to nowhere.

Children have great trouble imagining the inner lives of those in authority. A young school child can be deeply puzzled to see their teacher on a Sunday morning at the shops or jogging round the park. In their minds, this mighty person is simply and exclusively 'the teacher'. Their whole life (the child thinks) revolves around the classroom and the large desk they stand behind. They have no history; they couldn't have been a child themselves; they have no problems or frustrated dreams or wakeful nights. Our childish selves struggle to flesh out the reality of adult existence.

However, maturity means, ideally, going from the myth of a person, however high their status in a system, to a full recognition of their humanity. We finally pay others a strange but valid compliment when we accept them as versions of the same complex and imperfect creatures we know ourselves to be. This may feel like disenchantment, but it is also a crucial vehicle for a future in which the word 'no' seems just a little less impartial and beyond question.

V

History is Now

One of the things that separates confident from diffident people is their approach to history. Broadly speaking, the unconfident believe that history is over; conversely, the confident trust that history is still in the process of being made – and possibly by themselves one day.

The way we enter the world carries with it an inherent bias towards an impression that history has been settled. Everything around us conspires to convey a sense that the status quo is entrenched. We are surrounded by people far taller than us, who follow traditions that have been in place for decades – centuries, even. Our understanding of time hugely overprivileges the immediate moment. To a five-year-old, last year feels like a century ago. The house we live in appears as immutable as an ancient temple; the school we go to looks as though it has been performing the same rituals since the earth began. We are constantly told why things are the way they are and encouraged to accept that reality is not made according to our wishes. We come to trust that human beings have fully mapped the range of the possible. If something hasn't happened, it's either because it can't happen, or it shouldn't.

The result is a deep wariness around imagining alternatives. There is no point starting a new business (the market must be full already), pioneering a new approach to the arts (everything is already set in a fixed pattern), or giving loyalty to a new idea (it either exists or is mad).

When we study history, however, the picture changes sharply. Once time is speeded up and we climb up a mountain of minutes to survey the centuries, change appears constant. New continents are discovered; alternative ways of governing nations are pioneered; ideas of how to dress and who to worship are transformed. Once people wore strange cloaks and tilled the land with clumsy instruments. A long time ago, they chopped off a king's head. Way back, people got around in fragile ships, ate the eyeballs of sheep, used chamber pots and didn't know how to fix teeth.

We come away from all this knowing, in theory at least, that things do change. However, in practice, and almost without noticing, we tend to distance ourselves and our own societies from a day-to-day belief that we belong to the same ongoing turbulent narrative and are, at present, its central actors. History, we feel, is what used to happen; it can't really be what is happening around us in the here and now. In our vicinity at least, things have settled down.

To attenuate this insensitivity to the omnipresence of change, and by extension the passivity it breeds, we might turn to some striking lines in T.S. Eliot's cycle of poems, *The Four Quartets* (1943):

> So, while the light fails
> On a winter's afternoon, in a secluded chapel
> History is now and England.

Winter afternoons, around 4pm, have a habit of feeling particularly resolved and established, especially in quiet English country chapels, many of which date back to the middle ages. The air in such chapels is still and musty. The heavy stone floors have been slowly worn away by the feet of the faithful. There might be a leaflet advertising an upcoming concert and a charity box hoping to catch our eye. Over the altar, a stained-glass window of the saints (Peter and John, holding a lamb each) glows from the last of the light. These are not places and times to think about changing the world; everything hints that we would be wiser to accept the way things are, walk back home across the fields, light a fire and settle down for the evening. Hence the surprise of Eliot's third line, his resonant: 'History is now and England.'

In other words, everything that we associate with history – the impetuous daring of great people, the dramatic alterations in values, the revolutionary questioning of long-held beliefs, the upturning of the old order – is still going on, even at this very moment, in outwardly peaceful, apparently unchanging places like the countryside near Shamley Green, in Surrey, where Eliot wrote the poem. We don't see it only because we are standing too close to it. The world is being made and remade in every instant. Therefore, any one of us has a theoretical chance of being an agent in history, on a big or a small scale. It is open to our own times to build a new city as beautiful as Venice; to change ideas as radically as the Renaissance; to start an intellectual movement as resounding as Buddhism.

The present has all the contingency of the past, and is every bit as malleable. It should not intimidate us. How we love, travel, approach the arts, govern, educate ourselves, run businesses, age and die are all up for further development. Current views may appear firm, but only because we exaggerate their fixity. The majority of what exists is arbitrary, neither inevitable nor right, simply the result of muddle and happenstance. We should be confident, even at sunset on winter afternoons, of our power to join the stream of history and, however modestly, change its course.

The majority
of what exists
is arbitrary,
the result of
muddle and
happenstance.

VI
Experience

One of the greatest sources of despair is the belief that things should have been easier than they have turned out to be. We give up not simply because events are difficult, but because we hadn't expected them to be so. The struggle is interpreted as humiliating proof that we do not have the talent required to carry out our wishes. We grow subdued and timid and eventually surrender, because a struggle this great seems impossibly rare.

The capacity to remain confident is, therefore, to a significant extent a matter of having internalised a correct narrative about what difficulties we are likely to encounter. Unfortunately, the narratives we have to hand are deeply misleading, for a range of reasons. We are surrounded by stories that conspire to make success seem easier than it is, and therefore that unwittingly destroy the confidence we can muster in the face of our obstacles.

Some of the explanations for the preponderance of optimistic narratives are benign. If we told a small child what lay in store for them – the loneliness, the fractious relationships, the unfulfilling jobs – they might cave in and give up. We prefer to read them the adventures of Miffy, the adorable bunny.

At other points, the reasons for the silence around difficulty are slightly more self-serving: we are trying to impress people. The successful artist or skilled entrepreneur go to great lengths to disguise their labours and make their work appear simple, natural and obvious. 'Art lies in concealing art,' opined the Roman poet Horace.

The great stand-up comic does not reveal the time spent agonising over every detail of their performance. They will not tell us of the anxieties around whether it was best to deliver the last line sitting, to convey an impression of stunned passivity, or standing, to imply a stifled energy about to be released; or whether it was preferable to use the word 'tiny' or simply go with 'very, very small' as the punchline to the opening joke. Appearing to say the first thing that comes into one's head is the result of decades of rehearsal.

As customers, we pay to have news of struggle kept from us. We don't wish to read the novelist's early drafts; we don't want to hear about the company's difficulties in setting up the hotel or the engineer's complaints about the hydraulic system. We want to admire the polished surface of the gadget without reminder of the cramped circuits beneath.

The great stand-up comic does not reveal the time spent agonising over every detail of their performance.

But there comes a point, when we move from consumers to producers, that we start to pay in heightened currency for our ignorance; the currency of confidence and self-respect. We see our early failures as proof of conclusive ineptness rather than as the inevitable stages on every path to mastery. Without an accurate developmental map, we can't position ourselves properly with regards to our defeats. We have not seen enough of the rough drafts of those we admire, and therefore cannot forgive ourselves the horror of our own early attempts.

Certain societies have been wiser than our own in communicating the challenges of all noble endeavours. For instance, the ancient temple dedicated to the Goddess Aphaia, on the Greek island of Aegina, was decorated with prominent pieces of sculpture that set out to portray a very precise idea of what your life would be like as a warrior. Someone would try to stab you with a spear; the person standing next to you in the phalanx would collapse; you'd be pushed over backwards, bash your head with your own sword and a determined adversary would probably fire an arrow in your back as you turned to flee.

Those who commissioned the temple were deliberately preparing their people for the hardships of battle, so they

The statues in Aegina's Temple of Aphaia showed the gritty realities of warfare to prepare soldiers for the battlefield.

would be ready when they entered the field. At the same time, they were dignifying the lives of those who dared undergo these titanic struggles. The warriors deserved prestige, the temple builders were saying, because war was never a route to easy glory. It was imperative that such statuary not be hidden away but displayed right in the centre of town, so that one would encounter it on serious and important occasions from youth onwards. Despite their limited resources, ancient Greek communities went to astonishing lengths to remind themselves of what the most prestigious job available actually involved: namely, a lot of hardship.

We are, by contrast, recklessly short on detailed, honest and compelling accounts of what to expect around key aspects of our professional lives. To shore up our confidence, we would need regularly to encounter the modern equivalents of the works of the classical sculptors: films, poems, songs and novels that would represent for us the agonies that unfold in the unglamorous but hugely representative hubs of modern capitalism; the world's distribution centres, tax offices, airport lounges, HR conferences and management retreats.

The confidence-boosting artists would show us, without

reserve or coyness, what a successful life truly involves. They would take us through the tears we will shed in office cubicles; the meetings in which our ideas will be rejected and our projections thwarted; the mocking articles we will read about ourselves in newspapers; the hours we'll spend in lonely foreign hotel rooms while we miss out on our children's school plays; the sense that our best insights have arrived far too late; the inability to sleep from worry and confusion.

Thereby, we'd be better placed to meet our own eventual experiences against a realistic set of expectations. Our setbacks would take on a different meaning. Instead of looking like confidence-destroying evidence of our incapacities, they would much more readily strike us as proof that we were on the standard path to what we admire. We'd interpret our worries, reversals and troubles as unavoidable landmarks, not aberrations or fateful warnings.

Confidence isn't the belief that we won't meet obstacles: it is the recognition that difficulties are an inescapable part of all worthwhile contributions. We need to ensure we have plenty of narratives to hand that normalise the role of pain, anxiety and disappointment in even the best and most successful lives.

VII
Death

There is so much that we put off every day: the relationship that, for the sake of both participants, it would be better to end; the new person it would be thrilling to get close to; the alternative career that promises to utilise our deepest talents; the house with the beautiful views over water. And yet we do nothing. There may be distressed moments of recognition at three in the morning, but in the light of day we bury our longings and muddle on. We find ourselves musing on the interesting things we'll do when we retire. We let life leak away.

Our hesitation is grounded in a sense of risk. Every move presents us with appalling dangers. The new house might not be right; the change of career might lead to ruin; the beloved might reject us; we could regret leaving the old relationship. But our inaction is not in itself cost-free, for in the wings, out of regular conscious awareness, there is something arguably even more frightening than failure: the tragedy of wasting our lives.

We too easily ignore the most stupid yet deepest fact about our existence: that it will end. The brutal fact of our mortality seems so implausible that we live in practical terms like immortals, as if we will always have the opportunity to address our stifled longings one day.

Frans Hals, *Young Man Holding a Skull*, 1626.

This painting typifies the genre of the *Vanitas* – a reminder of the

fleetingness of life, usually featuring a skull.

There will be time next year, or the year after. But by hyping up the dangers of failure in action, we underrate the seriousness of the dangers lurking within passivity. In comparison with the horror of our final exit, the pains and troubles of our bolder moves and riskier ventures do not, in the end, seem so terrifying. We should learn to frighten ourselves a bit more in one area to be less scared in others.

It is hardly surprising that we struggle with the notion of how long we will be here. At first, life seems quite endless. At seven, it feels like an eternity till Christmas. At eleven, it is almost impossible to imagine what it might be like to be twenty-two. At twenty-two, thirty feels absurdly remote. Time does us a disservice in seeming so long, and yet turning out to be so resolutely short. Typically, people only become gripped by the idea of mortality at a few select points in their lives. Turning forty or fifty can bring a sudden reversal of perspective. We panic or become morose. We buy a new car or take up a musical instrument. However, what this really indicates is a dramatic failure of anticipation. The extraordinary aspect is not that we're dying, but that the reality of the nature of existence did not get fixed firmly enough in our brains at an earlier, more appropriate, moment. A mid-life crisis is not a legitimate awakening; it's a sign of being shamefully ill prepared.

We should never need to be awoken. In an ideal culture, our mortality would be systematically impressed upon us from the earliest age. There would be a specific day each month when everyone attended a stranger's funeral. Every news bulletin would be followed by a live feed from a hospice. Career guidance would start with a brief meditation on the preponderance of heart attacks and pancreatic cancers. We'd have impressively grim monuments across our cities (in supermarket car parks and around football stadia): 'To Those Who Wasted Their Lives'. Worrying about where life was going would be treated as an admirable and important characteristic. You'd often overhear people saying: 'I really like X; they're so concerned about wasting their life.'

Even without this ideal society-wide support there are moves we can make ourselves to usefully intensify our awareness of our own limited spans: we should assemble our own repertoire of reminders, perhaps a skull, a set of cancer statistics or a close-up of the sort of capillary that can unleash a stroke.

We need regular, forceful encounters with reminders that there is something else we should be far more frightened of than embarrassment around holding someone's hand or a bit of trouble as we change the subject of our university degree.

VIII
Enemies

Learning that someone hates us deeply, even though we have done nothing ostensibly to provoke them, can be one of the most alarming situations we face. At a bar after work, we might be told, via a malevolent third party, that two people in the office deem us arrogant and disrespectful and that, for the last few months, they haven't lost a chance to put us down behind our backs. Or we might learn that a friend of a friend, a senior professor, has forceful objections to a paper of ours; they called it 'naive' and 'stuck in the 1970s' and made sarcastic jokes at our expense at a conference. Furthermore, because of technology, we're now aware of a vast new range of potential enemies scattered around the digital universe. We are only ever a few seconds of online searching away from pitiless, personally targeted assessments of all that we are.

For the underconfident among us, enemies are a catastrophe. In our psychological make-up, the approval of the world effectively supports our approval of ourselves. Consequently, when enemies agitate against us, we lose faith not in them (they continue to exert a mesmeric authority over us), but, more alarmingly, in ourselves. We may, when with our friends, casually profess to hate the haters (and curse their names with bravado), but in private, over the ensuing months, we simply cannot dismiss their judgements, because we have accorded them a status logically prior to our own in our deep minds. Their objections may feel unbearable, like a physical discomfort we cannot correct, but we can't reject them as unwarranted either. In despair, it feels as if we do not know how to carry on, not only because we've been called idiots or egotists, but because, as a result, we must simply be idiots and egotists.

The judgements of others have been given a free pass to enter all the rooms of our minds. There is no one manning the border between them and us: the enemies are freely in us, wandering wildly and destructively through the caverns of our inner selves, ripping items off the shelves and mocking everything we are. In our distress, we may keep harping back to the idea (it brings tears to our eyes) that the situation is profoundly 'unfair': we did nothing especially wrong, our intentions are benevolent and our work is acceptable. Why, therefore, has our name been trampled upon and our reputation trashed? Either because we truly are fools (which is an unendurable truth) or because we're not fools (in which case the hatred is an unendurable error). Whatever is right, we can't just walk away and get on with our lives. We feel compelled to take some kind of corrective action to scrub away the stain our enemies have applied. In the middle of the night, we contemplate a range of responses: angry, passive-aggressive, self-harming, charming, begging.... Our partner might implore us to drop it and return to bed. We cannot: the enemy refuses to leave our heads.

Where does such underconfidence around enemies come from? We should, as ever, begin with parents and sketch an imaginary portrait of types who could unwittingly create such tortured mindsets. However ostensibly loving these parents might have been, they are also likely to have felt a high degree of trust in the system. If the police were investigating one of their friends, their guess would be that the authorities were correct in their suspicions. When reading a newspaper, if they were to read a destructive review of a novel, even one by an author whose work they'd much enjoyed in the past, it would seem evident that the author had lost his talent and was now kidding the public. If the parents were friends with an architect who was up for a major prize that was then awarded to somebody else, they'd feel the friend – whose buildings they admired – must have lacked talent in comparison with the winner, whose dark asymmetrical structures they would vow at once to take a second, more respectful, look at.

When it came to their own children, these underconfidence-generating parents would have applied a similar method of judgement: the issue of how much and where to love would have been to a large extent determined externally. If the world felt the baby was adorable, they probably were (and if not, then not so much). Later, if the child won a maths prize, it was a sign not just of competence at algebra but of being, far more broadly, a love-worthy person. Conversely, if the school report described the child as an easily distracted dreamer who looked as if he would flunk his exams, that might mean the offspring didn't quite deserve to exist. The lovability of the child in the eyes of the parents rose and fell in accordance with the respect, interest and approval of the world.

To be on the receiving end of such parenting is a heavy burden. We, the recipients of conditional love, have no option but to work manically to fulfil the conditions set up by parental and worldly expectations. Success isn't simply a pleasant prize to stumble upon when we enjoy a subject or a task interests us; it is a psychological necessity, something we must secure in order to feel we have the right to be alive. We don't have any memories of success-independent affection and therefore constantly need to recharge our batteries from the external power source of the world's flickering and wilful interest. Unsurprisingly, when enemies come on the horizon, we are quickly in deep trouble, for we have no ability to hold in our minds the concept that they might be wrong and we right; that our achievements are not our being, and that the failure of our actions does not presuppose failure of our entire selves. Rendered defenceless by our upbringing, we have no border post between inside and out. We are at the mercy of pretty much anyone who might decide to hate us.

Contrast this with the blessed childhood of the confident. Their parents would have maintained a vigorously sceptical relationship to the system. The world might sometimes be right, but then again, on key occasions, it could be gravely and outrageously wrong. Everyone was, in their eyes, endowed with their own capacity to judge. It is not because the crowd is jeering that the accused is guilty, or vice versa. The chief of police, the lead reviewer of The Times, or the head of the Pritzker Architecture Prize might well be idiotic; these things happen. In their role as parents, the messages of the confidence-inducing were no less generous in their scepticism: 'You are loved in and of yourself because of what you are, not what you do.

You aren't always admirable or even likeable, but you are always deserving of affection and charity of interpretation. It doesn't matter to me if you end up the president or the street cleaner. You will always be something more important: my child. If they don't have the wisdom to be kind, fuck them!'. Without necessarily intending this, the parents set up a soothing voice that still plays on a loop in the recesses of the mind, especially at moments of greatest challenge. It is the voice of love.

We cannot go back and change the past that made us. However, by understanding the structure of what we are missing, we may at least strive to integrate emotionally healthier voices into our agitated interiors. The verdict of the system is never totally wrong, but nor is it ever more than occasionally right: police forces get muddled; reviewers redirect their disappointments onto innocent targets; prize committees fall under the sway of fashion. The world doesn't reliably 'know'. We cannot change the presence of an enemy, but we can change what an enemy means to us. These figures can shift from being devoted, impartial agents of truth about one's right to exist to being – more sanely – people who have an opinion, probably only ever a bit right, about something we once did, and never about who we are (that is something we decide).

Panicking about having acquired a few enemies can be a symptom of a dangerous trust in human beings as a whole. Underconfident types work with the assumption that almost everyone they encounter will be sane, measured, intelligent, judicious, and in command of themselves. If, despite these attributes, certain people still write nasty things online or describe us as a nuisance, the attacks simply have to be true. Yet the more psychologically robust are saved from such dispiriting assumptions by a highly useful skill: fierce pessimism. They assume from the start that most people, even grand and supposedly intelligent ones, are riddled with prejudice, beset by low motives, and capable of deliberate cattiness and meanness better suited to a playground of the under-fives. They lie, they slander, they project, they say things to make themselves feel better, they are envious and inadequate, cruel and close to evil. Why should we be surprised and disturbed if a few people happen to be nasty to us, given that nastiness is more or less the fundamental truth of human nature? The benefit of thinking a lot less of everyone can be a calmer attitude towards the specific meanness of a few.

Armed with darker thoughts, the confident know that every decent and interesting person is going to accumulate a string of enemies as they make their way through life. It would be impossible for it to be otherwise, given human nature. The specific reasons will be varied and somewhat random: some of these enemies will flare up because they have vested interests in a status quo we are challenging; some may be uncomfortably reminded of their own renounced ambitions when they encounter our skills; some may find our achievements humiliating to their sense of self-worth; some are people who might have wanted to be our friends or even our lovers, and then turned sour when this proved impossible. We will constantly be the target of anger, but we don't have to believe ourselves to be its true cause.

In the 17th century, the Dutch developed a tradition of painting ships in violent storms. These works, which hung in private homes and in municipal buildings around the Dutch republic, were not mere decoration. They had an explicitly therapeutic purpose: they delivered a moral to their viewers, who lived in a nation critically dependent on maritime trade, about confidence in seafaring and life more broadly. The sight of a tall sailing ship being tossed to a twenty-degree angle in a rough sea looks like a catastrophe to an inexperienced person. But there are many situations that look and feel much more dangerous than they really are, especially when the

Ludolf Bakhuysen, *Warships in a Heavy Storm*, c. 1695.

crew is prepared and the ship internally sound. Consider Ludolf Bakhuysen's work *Warships in a Heavy Storm*. The scene looks chaotic in the extreme: how could they possibly survive? But the ships were well designed for just such situations. Their hulls had been minutely adapted through long experience to withstand the tempests of the northern oceans. The crews practised again and again the manoeuvres that could keep their vessels safe: they knew how to take down sails at speed and ensure that the wind would not shred the mast. They understood about shifting cargo in the hull, tacking to the left and then abruptly to the right, and pumping out water from the inner chambers. They knew how to remain coolly scientific in responding to the storm's wilful, frantic motions. The picture pays homage to decades of planning and experience. One can imagine the older sailors on the ship saying to a terrified novice, with a laugh, that just last year off the coast of Jutland there was an even bigger storm – and slapping him on the back with paternal playfulness as the youth was sick overboard. Bakhuysen wanted us to feel proud of humanity's resilience in the face of apparently dreadful challenges. His painting enthuses us with the message that we can all cope far better than we think; that what appears immensely threatening may be highly survivable.

What is true of storms in the North Sea may be no less true of enemies at the office. Their aggression can be terrifying, like the giant waves off Den Helder, yet in reality – with deft emotional skill and internal reorganisation – can prove eminently manageable. The storms are not really about us, and we can survive them by refusing to let the verdicts of others become our verdicts on ourselves. We should keep in mind a confident distinction between the hater and the critic, aim to correct our genuine flaws, and otherwise forgive the injured, roaring winds that seek to punish us for pressures that have nothing to do with us. The storms will die down, we will be battered, a few things will be ripped, but eventually we will return to safer shores – as the sun rises over the spires of Alkmaar.

IX

Self-Sabotage

It is normal to expect that we will always – almost by nature – actively seek our own happiness, especially in two big areas of potential satisfaction: relationships and careers.

It is therefore odd and a little unnerving to find how often many of us act as if we were deliberately out to ruin our chances of getting what we want. When going on dates with candidates we are keen on, we may lapse into unnecessarily opinionated and antagonistic behaviour. When we are in a relationship with someone we love, we may drive them to distraction through repeated unwarranted accusations and angry explosions, as if we were somehow willing to bring on the sad day when, exhausted and frustrated, the beloved would be forced to walk away, still sympathetic but unable to take our elevated degree of suspicion and drama.

Similarly, we might be led to destroy our chances of a major promotion at work when, just after giving a particularly convincing presentation to the board, we grow bizarrely strident with the CEO or become drunk and insulting at a crucial client dinner.

Such behaviour can't be put down to mere bad luck. It

deserves a stronger, more intentional term: self-sabotage. We are familiar enough with the fear of failure, but it appears that success can sometimes bring about as many anxieties, which may ultimately culminate in a desire to scupper our chances in a bid to restore our peace of mind.

What could possibly explain this suspicion of success? In certain cases, an unconscious desire to protect those who love us, particularly those who cared for us in childhood, from a sense of envy and inadequacy that might be triggered by our gains. The beautiful new partner or the promotion to a senior role may prove silently devastating to those around us, prompting them to wonder about how little they have achieved by comparison and to fear that they will be deemed no longer good enough to merit our company.

It can feel odd to accept that those who loved us as children could harbour envious feelings towards us, especially when they might be devoted to us in most other ways. Yet these caregivers may nevertheless be carrying a private layer of regret within them about the course of their own lives and attendant fears of being neglected and thought unimportant by others, even their own children. As we were growing up, there might have been telling reminders about not getting too big for one's boots and not forgetting where one came from, disguised pleas not to be forgotten and overlooked. We can end up in a bind: the success we long for threatens to hurt the feelings of those we love.

The solution, once we discover the impasse, is not to sabotage ourselves; it is to grow deeply generous and proactive around the real reasons why our caregivers could have ended up feeling so apprehensive about our achievements. We should recognise that these caregivers are not, ultimately, afraid of our success so much as they are afraid of being abandoned and reminded of their own inadequacies. The task, therefore, isn't to ruin our chances; it is to try to reassure our nervous companions of our essential loyalty and of their primordial value.

A second common type of self-saboteur is one who finds the price of hope too high to pay. When we were younger, we may have been exposed to exceptionally brutal disappointments at a time when we were too fragile to withstand them. Perhaps we hoped our parents would stay together and they didn't. Or we hoped our father would eventually come back from another country and stay. Perhaps we dared to love someone and, after a few weeks of happiness, they swiftly and oddly changed their attitude and mocked us in front of our peers. Somewhere in our characters, a deep association has been forged between hope and danger, along with a corresponding preference to live quietly with disappointment rather than more freely with hope.

The solution is to remind ourselves that we can, despite our fears, survive the loss of hope. We are no longer those who suffered the disappointments responsible for our present timidity. The conditions that forged our caution are no longer those of adult reality. The unconscious mind may, as is its wont, be reading the present through the lenses of decades ago, but what we fear will happen has, in truth, already happened; we are projecting into the future a catastrophe that belongs to a past we have not had the chance to fathom and mourn adequately.

Furthermore, what fundamentally distinguishes adulthood from childhood is that the adult has access to a great many more sources of hope than the child. We can survive a letdown here or there, because we no longer inhabit a closed province, bounded by the family, the neighbourhood and the school. We can use the whole world as an orchard in which to nurture a diversity of hopes that will always outstrip the inevitable, yet only ever occasional and survivable, crushing disappointment.

Lastly, we may destroy success from touching modesty: from the sense that we cannot really deserve the bounty we have received. We may turn to consider our new job or lover in the light of all the sides of ourselves that we know to be less than perfect – our laziness, cowardice, stupidity and immaturity – and conclude that there must have been a mistake and that we must therefore return our gifts to the more deserving. But this is kindly, though balefully, to misunderstand the way success and pain are allotted. The universe does not distribute its gifts and its horrors with divinely accurate knowledge of the good and bad within each of us. Most of what we win is not quite deserved and most of what we suffer isn't either. Cancer wards are not filled with the exceptionally wicked.

When we feel oppressed by a sense of not meriting our favours, we need only remind ourselves that we will soon enough not deserve our maledictions either. Our diseases, public falls from grace and romantic abandonments will in time be as undeserved as our beauty, elevations and loving partners might now be. We should not worry so much about the latter, nor complain

We can,
despite our
fears, survive
the loss
of hope.

quite so bitterly about the former. We should accept from the start, with good grace and dark premonition, the sheer randomness and amorality of fate.

It can be useful to keep the concept of self-sabotage in mind when interpreting our and others' odder antics. We should start to get suspicious when we catch ourselves pulling off erratic performances around people we deep down really like or need to impress.

Furthermore, faced with certain kinds of viciousness and unreliability in others, we should dare to imagine that things are not quite as they seem; we might have on our hands not a malevolent opponent, but an almost touchingly wounded self-saboteur, who chiefly deserves a little patience and should gently be coaxed out of doing themselves further harm.

We should come to terms with, and help others to see, just how hard and unnerving it can sometimes be to get close to the things we truly want.

X

Confidence in Confidence

Although we assume that we, like everyone else, must want to be confident, we may harbour private suspicions that confidence is in fact an unappealing state of mind. We might, without fully realising it, find the idea of being truly confident strangely offensive, and secretly remain attached to hesitancy and modesty.

We may take quiet pride in the fact that we aren't the types to complain in restaurants. We don't kick up a fuss about our salary. We don't ask all our friends to rearrange their holidays for our sakes. We don't play our music loudly. Our meekness protects us from some deeply off-putting associations around self-assertion. These might have been forged early on in our lives in the presence of people who were both hugely unpleasant and highly certain of their right to exist. They may have been terrifyingly demanding, impatient, dismissive and brash. They might have shouted in service situations and slammed the phone down on people they believed didn't respect them enough. We may have started to think that this is how people needed to behave in order to succeed and that if this were the case, then conspicuous success wouldn't be for us.

We shouldn't forget that suspicion of confidence has

traditionally enjoyed immense cultural endorsement. Christianity, for centuries the greatest influence on the mindset of the West, was highly sceptical about those might think too well of themselves. While the meek basked in divine favour, the arrogant would be the last to enter the kingdom of heaven. The political theory of Karl Marx (1818–1883) added to this argument a set of theories apparently proving that economic success was always founded upon the exploitation of others. No wonder it may feel as if, to be moral citizens, we should steer clear of all overly robust assertions of our own interests.

Yet this attitude too can carry dangers. We may lack the confidence not to be cruel and promote idiocy, but to fight for kindness and wisdom. Our lack of confidence in confidence may allow degraded versions of self-assertion to thrive.

Our attitude may also be unfair. Our negative view of confidence may be overly dependent on the quirks of our own histories, on the sort of people we first encountered confidence in who were not its best or most reliable representatives. Our real problem may not be confidence so much as a lack of other virtues such as manners, charm, wit and generosity. We may be wrongly diagnosing the root of our objections. There may be a few people at risk of growing into braggarts, self-seekers and blowhards. But confidence is in its essence entirely compatible with remaining sensitive, kind, witty and softly-spoken. It might be brutishness, not confidence, that we hate.

Furthermore, our attraction to meekness may mask some cowardly resentment against self-assertion. We might not so much admire timidity as fear trying confidence. It was this species of self-protective deception that particularly fascinated the German philosopher Nietzsche (1844–1900). He thought it a typical error of many Christians, who might pride themselves on their 'forgiveness' while in reality simply trying to excuse their 'inability to take revenge'. We should take care not to dress up our base deficiencies as godly virtues.

Unfortunately it isn't enough to be kind, interesting, intelligent and wise *inside*: we need to develop the skill that allows us to make our talents active in the world at large. Confidence is what translates theory into practice. It should never be thought of as the enemy of good things; it is their crucial and legitimate catalyst. We should allow ourselves to develop confidence in confidence.

Credits

95

The School of Life publishes a range of books on essential topics in psychological and emotional life, including relationships, parenting, friendship, careers and fulfilment. The aim is always to help us to understand ourselves better – and thereby to grow calmer, less confused and more purposeful. Discover our full range of titles, including books for children, here:

www.theschooloflife.com/books

The School of Life also offers a comprehensive therapy service, which complements, and draws upon, our published works:

www.theschooloflife.com/therapy